Novel Writing for Beginners

Guidance From An Editor

By Beth Frances Cox

For Geraldine,

Who learned the hard way that like the blues, "…it don't come easy."

How to Write a Novel
A Mystery
Or a spy thriller
A romance, a fantasy
Or any novel, for that matter

A guide to planning, organizing and writing your book

By Beth Frances Cox
Copyright 2020 Beth Frances Inc.
Cover design by Tyler LeBlanc

Topics Covered

General Thoughts
On Bad Writing
Plots
Keep a Notebook
Dialogue
First Person?
Locale
Write Every Day
Let's Talk dirty
Writing Tech
Out of Town Words
Dictation
Style
Titles
The Writing Community
List your characters
The Heart of the Matter
Form of an Outline
Epigraph
Prologue
That First Sentence
Getting Started
Sample outline, Chapter 1
Sample outline, Chapter 2
Sample outline, Chapter 3
Sample outline, Chapter 4
Sample outline, Chapter 5
Sample outline, Chapter 6

Sample outline, Chapter 7
Sample outline, Chapter 8
Sample outline, Chapter 27
Sample outline, Epilogue
OK, Get Writing
Keep Going
First Drafts
What's That Mean?
The Editing Process
Marketing Your Book
Recommended Reading
A few Words on Plagiarism
Those Pesky Commas
Is This Worth Doing?
One More Thing

Preface

"This is how you do it: you sit down at the keyboard and you put one word after another until it's done. It's that easy, and that hard."
—Neil Gaiman

There are two kinds of novel writers in this world, Outliners and Pantsers.

This book is for Outliners.

Pantsers—also known as those who just wing it— are those gifted folks who can do it by the seat of their pants, who can keep it all in their head, who go along and seemingly write, write, write almost effortlessly. For them, it all comes out polished in the end, with very little editing needed.

There are a few great talents like this out there. If you can do it like that, you don't need this book. Give it to a friend.

For the rest of us, writing a novel is a process best approached with an outline. You'll need to bring some organizational skills to go along with that great plot involving those fascinating characters, the ones you've been thinking about for months or years.

This book is intended to help aspiring writers get started constructing something readable— maybe not The Great American Novel, but at least a serviceable beach read and maybe even a series of works that can bring you a steady income stream.

Think of what follows as a framework, a blueprint, an easy way to outline your project by breaking it down into a series of small steps.

Don't get this wrong— there's no substitute for good writing, a great turn of phrase, fascinating characters, witty dialogue, plot twists, descriptive, scene-setting paragraphs. That part is up to you. But if you've got a novel in you and you want to get it out, if you've ever become bogged down, or don't know where to start, here's a good explanation of how and where to begin.

We recommend you read what follows all the way through, maybe even several times. Take a few notes. You can follow the steps laid out here and probably produce a decent piece of prose.

Here's how to get started.

First, Some General Thoughts

"Read, read, read. Read everything— trash, classics, good and bad, and see how they do it. Just like a carpenter who works as an apprentice and studies the master. Read! You'll absorb it. Then write. If it's good, you'll find out. If it's not, throw it out the window."
—**William Faulkner**

On Bad Writing

Why is there so much bad writing out there?

For author and psychologist Steven Pinker, the root cause of so much bad writing is what he calls "the curse of knowledge," which he defines as "a difficulty in imagining what it is like for someone else not to know something that you know. The curse of knowledge is the single best explanation I know of why good people write bad prose."

Why so many bad novels out there today? It may be that you know your story so well that you have trouble putting yourself in the mind's eye of the reader. After all, you've been thinking about this book you're writing for months, maybe years. Not so your reader.

"I read my final draft pretending I'm someone else, just to make sure that what I've written makes sense from outside."
—**Anne Tyler**, *author of* The Accidental Tourist, Breathing Lessons *and many other novels*

Now, there used to be gate-keepers—agents and publishing house editors who could screen out most of the junk. There's a reason why traditional publishers call that stack of unsolicited manuscripts "the slush pile." (Today, it may be an overflowing email account.)

But times have changed. The fact that you can publish on your own, without an editor or an agent or even a proofreader, has significantly altered the book business, and not necessarily for the better. Look through a bunch of listings on Amazon, in almost any e-book category, and you'll find a lot of junk that's not worth the 99 cents they're charging for it. And, can you even trust the reviews? So, let's learn how to do it a little better than the hacks churning out dollar novels. Or maybe a lot better.

Plots

"Thick plots are my specialty. If you want a thinner kind, look elsewhere."
— **Margaret Atwood**, *author of The Handmaid's Tale.*

Yeah, you probably need one.

Some folks say that at its simplest, there are only three basic plots: happy ending, unhappy ending and tragedy. Seems like tragedy would be unhappy, so maybe there are only two.

One of the unhappiest endings of all time:

"After a while I went out and left the hospital and walked back to the hotel in the rain."
--**Ernest Hemingway**, *"A Farewell to Arms:"*

Here's one of the happiest:

"But wherever they go, and whatever happens to them on the way, in that enchanted place on the top of the Forest a little boy and his Bear will always be playing."
—**A.A. Milne**, *The House At Pooh Corner,*

Other folks say there are six plots: rags to riches, riches to rags, man in a hole (fall–rise), Icarus (rise–fall), Cinderella (rise–fall–rise), and Oedipus (fall–rise–fall).

Some folks have counted the number of plots up into the 30s or 40s, even the hundreds, including the fight against evil, journey and return (The Odyssey) overcoming the monster or beating the odds (Beowulf) or the quest, a search for something (can you say Indiana Jones?)

Regardless, you need a plot, and it's probably a good idea to think about that before you start any serious writing.

One way to start considering your plot is to boil it down, maybe using as a template some movies that you have enjoyed, to see if you have anything similar in mind.

For example:
 "Casablanca" – boy gets girl, boy loses girl, boy kind of gets girl, boy loses girl.
"Notting Hill" – Boy gets girl, boy loses girl, boy gets girl and so on.
"ET" – Alien falls to earth, gets help, goes home, i.e., a quest.
"Batman" – a fight against evil.
"Rocky" – Overcoming the odds.
"The Replacements" – Fall and then rise, or man in a hole.

Sometimes you can combine plots, as in the movie "Top Gun," where you see a rise, fall, rise hero who gets girl, loses girl, gets girl.

You should also think about (and even write down in your notebook—more on that later) the plots in books that you recently read and enjoyed.

"Moby Dick," for instance, is a quest plot. "Robinson Crusoe" is overcoming the odds.

Lots of more modern, literary books seem to have little in the way of plot, actually, and form a genre that one could almost call "slice of life," a technique used in many short stories and one that's sometimes expanded into novel-length treatises.

But that's not what we're about here. We just want to offer some help to get you started writing that mystery or adventure story you've always had in mind. Nothing fancy, just readable and entertaining— a story.

"The most important thing, the all-important thing, is to get the story right. Write, rewrite, rewrite again, and do not worry about anything except story. It is story, story, story… Once the story is right, everything else will follow."
—Bernard Cornwell

Remember though, a plot is just a bare-bones skeleton. You will need to add the creativity to make your characters come alive, to give them history, to describe the action, to set the scene, to write that sparkling dialogue.

And if you're writing a mystery, do take pains not to make it too easy for the reader to solve.

One other thought about plots. In the newspaper business, they ask reporters about the five Ws and the H — Who, What, Where, When, Why and How. As you consider your plot, it's a good way to boil it all down. You should write it out and refer back to it if you get lost. Try writing one single sentence to summarize your whole book.

Somewhere, down the road, if you get lost in your prose, maybe take a day or two off from writing, and then reread that single sentence.

Keep a Notebook

"Don't tell me the moon is shining; show me the glint of light on broken glass."
— ***Anton Chekhov***

Most writers keep a notebook with them almost all the time. You should, too. In it they jot down things they may have seen or heard, ideas that came out of the blue, overheard conversations, an interesting turn of phrase, words new to them, their dreams, something so beautifully written you wish you had written it.

They note anything that might come in handy somewhere down the road. Maybe paraphrased, maybe stood on its head. Maybe snatches of poetry.

Here are a few from a long list one writer has been keeping for a few years:

He was 8 years old and already he could give you a really good stink eye

Haptic

Synecdoche

There are people who love you dearly but just don't know how to show it.

I thought that love would last forever: I was wrong.
—W.H. Auden

She had the go-to-hell look of a young New York City lioness...

Syncretism

The best part of him ran down his mother's leg.

Smells like … God's vagina

Adventure is simply the pursuit of awe.

Red state, buck-toothed, scrotum-faced, daughter-fucking lizard people.

Digibabble

Cosplay

Moving through life, much abraded by time

That moment when you finally embrace New York City and make it yours:

"There is a way of walking in New York, midevening, in the big, blocky East Fifties, that causes the heart to open up and the entire city to rush in and make a small town there ... The city stops its painful tantalizing then, its elusiveness and tease suspended, it takes off its clothes and nestles wakefully, generously, next to you. It is there, it is yours, no longer outwitting you. And it is not scary at all, because you love it very much."
— "Like Life," by **Lorrie Moore**

And many, many more.

Not everything you write has to be 100 percent original. And a lot of times, you can take what you've heard and twist it a bit and give it new life.

For example, we've all heard that question, "On a scale of 1 to 10, how much does it hurt?"
Just recently we heard this turned into "On a scale of WTF to what-the-hell, where are you now?"

Original? Well, maybe not, but perhaps worth stealing at some point as you go along churning out words. If you write these things down, you can now and again go back and take a look, see if there's anything useful there. It can come in handy if you're stuck, and need a jolt to the imagination. Write down everything you like, from song lyrics to bits of poetry to simply well-turned phrases.

Here's another phrase we came across recently: "He had weapons-grade likability." It went right into the old notebook. You could probably use "weapons-grade" to describe nearly anything. Just don't overdo it.

Here's another: It was as if these people were "…living out a kind of revenge fantasy against thinking."

And one more: As patient as evolution.

Dialogue

"Good writing is the hardest form of thinking. It involves the agony of turning profoundly difficult thoughts into lucid form, then forcing them into the tight-fitting uniform of language, making them visible and clear."
— **Pat Conroy**, *author of "The Prince of Tides" and many other books*

To use quote marks or not to use quote marks?

To start each new quote as a new paragraph or not?

The truth is, it does not matter. Cormac McCarthy writes entire novels without a single quote mark.

What's important is that the reader always has a pretty good idea of who is talking. The last thing you want to do as a writer of popular novels is to make the dialogue so complicated, so intertwined, that the reader has to stop to puzzle out who's talking. As long as the reader knows who is speaking, and knows that these are intended to be spoken words, everything is fine. Don't sweat it.

This is why it's important to have two or three other people, if possible, read your novel to catch those little places where the reader comes to a full stop, scratches their head and starts to flip back to see who is talking. That's not good, especially for a popular novel as opposed to the literary kind.

Also, although it's nice not to have to use a string of "he saids" or "she saids" after every quote, you don't need to break your dictionary looking for alternatives. Often, no attribution is needed at all as long as it's clear who is talking. And many times, a simple "said" is just fine.

Once, when we were wracking our brain looking for a transition, a wise editor advised, "Hey, just use the world 'meanwhile.' It quickly takes the reader from here to there, without much effort. Simple and effective."

Not everything has to stand up and scream "I Have Been Written!"

You want to write conversationally, as if you or your characters are speaking to an old friend. Try to write the way people talk. Remember, you're writing fiction, not an essay or a term paper. And as you look back over your own work, it can help to read it aloud. Or have a friend read it to you.

Sometimes you'll want to use contractions. Sometimes not. Developing a good ear for dialogue is very helpful.

Good dialogue doesn't simply show who the characters are, it shows how they relate to one another.

Says **Dave King** in a 2016 online essay about the dialogue written by **Aaron Sorkin**, who did much of the amazing dialogue for the first few years of "The West Wing" on television:

"Most of what fills out bad dialogue is linguistic chaff — generic phrases, stock responses, speech without thought. Once you winnow this out, you will not only have something more succinct, you'll have something more authentic."

He goes on to write: "… you don't necessarily have to weed out every cliché. They are sometimes the best way to say something. Even when they aren't, people often use clichés in real life, so an occasional one gives your dialogue verisimilitude."

Verisimilitude seems like an out-of-town word to us, but you get the drift. We'll have more to say about "about-of-town" words later.

First Person or Third Person?

"Nobody ever became a writer just by wanting to be one."
—F. Scott Fitzgerald

First person (I, me, mine) is probably a little easier to write, and lots of good novels are written that way. The big "I" has the advantage of putting the reader in the center of the story, making it easier to identify with the principal character.

The biggest limitation of first person, however, is that everything in the book is presented through the main character's eyes. There's little room for action that is outside the purview of the main character. That can be somewhat limiting, even though you are allowed, even encouraged, to let the main character think along the lines of whatever you might want to discuss, anything from the degradation of the environment to how best to troll for fish off a slow-moving sailboat. That part is up to you. If you think you have something to say, say it. Many novels include some commentary on life in our time.

Third person (he, she, it) eliminates the perspective problem, and allows you to write about what other characters are doing and saying outside the scope of the main character or characters. A lot can be happening that's not in the immediate purview of the main character, and this makes it a whole lot easier.

Or, you can simply combine the two, using different chapters or even different sections inside a chapter.

Some experienced writers use a different chapter for different characters, and pull them all together at the end of the book, showing the reader how they all relate. William Gibson, the sci fi writer, is very good at that. It keeps the reader guessing a bit. It's a technique that requires quite good and interesting material for each group of characters. This technique also offers the opportunity for shorter chapters, which may help the reader and probably helps the writer as well. But we don't recommend that approach for beginners.

Other writers separate first-person sections from third person within a chapter with a line or two of white space. That's perfectly fine, too.

Keep in mind that many people read a novel a little at a time, maybe at breakfast or in bed at night before turning out the light, and they like to break off at the end of a chapter or a section. A little breathing room is a good thing. You don't always have to end each chapter as a cliff-hanger. Sometimes your reader wants to just roll over and go to sleep.

Locale

"A well-grounded sense of place is the challenge for the writer."
— Travel writer **Tom Miller**

It's probably always best to write about the territory you know, at least for your first book. Otherwise, you'll need to do a ton of research. Nebraska is different from San Francisco is different from northern Ohio is different from Vermont.

Feel free to use a few local colloquialisms, but try not to overdo it. They're not eating loose meat sandwiches in Miami. You can't get a decent Cuban sandwich in Tennessee. Or a lobster roll in New Mexico.

And get things right. Little details matter. Some of your readers will know the name of that street, and they will know that it doesn't intersect with that other street.

If you have the travel bug, or if your story calls for some good local information about a place you've never visited, feel free to head out to soak up some color, if you can afford it. Travel expenses for serious writers can be deducted as a business expense.

At first, you might want to stick to writing about things that you know. Or can research thoroughly.

One writer we know plans to spend a week or two on a towboat on the Mississippi River, because his plot involves a string of killings with the bodies washing up on the bank all down the river. Realism is important, even if you're writing fiction. If you've never seen a towboat rounding up a bunch of runaway barges in a six-knot current, you wouldn't believe it possible.

A young writer we know once came to us with an incredibly poorly written couple of chapters for a first novel. He knew nothing about his setting or his characters. But when we asked him to write something about himself, in the first person, his description of growing up in a broken home in a terrible neighborhood with addicted parents brought tears to our eyes. That was a locale and an experience he could describe.

Mark Twain wrote about life on the Mississippi. Hemingway wrote about Paris and bullfighting and fishing. They knew those locales because they had lived there. Maybe you know about life in a cramped New York City studio. Or on a ranch in Wyoming. Or what things are like in the Florida Panhandle. Feel free to use what you know to enhance your story.
Of course, there are alternative views. There always are, no?

Consider this by acclaimed author **Annie Proulx**: *"What I find to be very bad advice is the snappy little sentence, 'Write what you know.' It is the most tiresome and stupid advice that could possibly be given. If we write simply about what we know we never grow. We don't develop any facility for languages, or an interest in others, or a desire to travel and explore and face experience head-on. We just coil tighter and tighter into our boring little selves. What one should write about is what interests one."*

And despite having no experience of being a gay man in the rural West, she wrote one of the saddest stories we have ever read, "Brokeback Mountain." And won a Pulitzer for her novel "The Shipping News." Yes, Newfoundland interested her.

Write Every Day

"Try to develop actual work habits and, even though you have a busy life, try to reserve an hour, say, or more a day to write. Very good things have been written on an hour a day."
— **John Updike**

Yeah. You have to work at it. So, pick a time. Pick a place. Pick a goal. Number of words, number of sentences, number of paragraphs, an amount of time. But write something every day, even if it's only a few words. Remember, you can always go back and edit your work. Pick a small goal at first. Maybe 100 words. Then gradually step it up. Some writers of romance novels can crank out thousands of words a day, and produce four or five books a year. But probably not at first.

If you get stuck on a word —maybe you can't spell it, or don't know its exact meaning—just put a couple of asterisks down as placeholders. You can come back to it later. Don't let it slow you down.

It's helpful, but of course not necessary, to rid yourself of potential distractions. Shut off the phone, maybe even shut off the Internet. Pick a location where you do nothing but write. A home office is great. Close the door and tell family members not to disturb you except in an emergency.

Hemingway once suggested you start by writing one true sentence. He never really defined a "true sentence," but it undoubtedly was a sentence that works, that carries the story forward, that is true unto itself, in context.

Just write something, even if you know it's not the best you can do. Come back and make it better later on. That's the editing part of writing. It's often where the real work happens, especially for writers who like to spew out words by the thousands. And hey, there's nothing wrong with spewing words. Some of those words may be pretty good. If the muse moves you, spew away. And remember to show, not tell. Newspapers tell; novelists show.

We'll talk about editing a little later on.

Let's Talk Dirty

"When I have to face writing sex scenes, I sometimes feel like I'm getting undressed in public. I feel like my mother is watching; like everyone will think I do all the things I describe. Do you ever feel that way? Get over it."
— **Gwynn Scheltema**

How to handle sex scenes. Bet we have your attention now.

There are probably as many ways to handle sex scenes as there are positions in the Kama Sutra, but in general, they can be divided into three types. Keep in mind always that you're writing a mystery or a romance novel here, not erotica or porn. Nothing against either of the latter, but they are not what we're about.

So, Type One is the classic Hollywood fade-away, in which you basically get right up to the kissing and then simply fade into the next scene or chapter, allowing the reader to use his or her imagination. OK, so they made love. Got it. Been there, done that, don't need all the sweaty details.

Type Two provides a little more detail, but doesn't get right down to the ins and outs of it. Some heavy breathing, some significant touching, here, there, and maybe there.

Type Three is enough to get you hot and bothered. It resembles erotica but stops short of porn. And where that line is drawn, wise men and women have been debating for ages. Take the word of former Supreme Court Justice Potter Stewart on obscenity: ""I shall not today attempt further to define the kinds of material I understand to be embraced ... I know it when I see it."

You will, too.

Unless you're an experienced writer you probably want to use Type One, or Type Two at most. But do try to keep your sex scenes in context, so that they occur naturally from the narrative, in the right place at the right time. You will know when that is, or your editor will. Every scene should flow from the one before, smoothly, inexorably, naturally, just like good love-making. Unless, of course, you're writing about some sort of brutal sex act.

Writing Tech

"Writing is a medium of human communication that represents language with signs and symbols. For languages that utilize a writing system, inscriptions can complement spoken language by creating a durable version of speech that can be stored for future reference or transmitted across distance."
— **Wikipedia**

No, not tech writing, that's something else entirely. But writing technology has certainly advanced from the days of longhand scribbling or even banging on a typewriter. Ah, the trusty Underwood or Royal. You youngsters can Google them.

No, what we're talking about here is high tech stuff for writers—spelling and grammar programs, such as Scrivener or Grammarly. And dictation hardware and software such as Dragon or any app that produces text from your spoken words.

Scrivener
This online service uses a ring binder notebook metaphor that allows for ease of organization, but you can just as easily organize your book on your own. Scrivener does have a built-in outlining feature that some folks may find helpful. The app claims to "offer all the tools you need to craft your first draft, from nascent notion to final full stop." "Nascent notion" seems like a couple of out-of-town words to us, so maybe they need an editor. Anyway, they go on to say that "Scrivener won't tell you how to write—it simply provides everything you need to start writing and keep writing." The app says that "integrated outlining tools let you plan everything first or restructure later." We recommend planning first, but we know there's not one-size-fits-all when it comes to creativity. Just do a Google search for "Scrivener."

Grammarly
From grammar and spelling to style and tone, Grammarly claims to help you eliminate errors and find the perfect words to express yourself. It's no substitute for a good human editor, but as a starting

point for looking over your prose, it can help a bit. Probably good for catching those idiotic cell phone guess-the-right word mistakes.

Grammarly says it has a product for just about every kind of writing, including an online editor for drafting long documents, plus desktop apps and a Microsoft Office add-in if you prefer not to write in your browser. They say Grammarly Keyboard for iOS and Android keeps you looking polished even when you're writing from your phone. And there's a Grammarly browser extension, which checks your writing if you're posting on web sites. The basic version is free. We've seen both positive and negative reviews, so, as they say, your mileage may vary.

Grammarly uses an AI that analyzes each sentence and looks for ways to improve it, whether it's correcting a verb tense, suggesting a stronger synonym or offering a clearer sentence structure. You make the final decision. Just keep in mind that like most AIs, it may be somewhat lacking in the creative department.

Plot Factory
There's also this one, which describes itself as "an online story planner that lets writers plan, organize, and write stories and fictional universes."

There are lots of other competing applications out there, so if you like, do a search online. Just be aware that none of these will actually write your novel for you. Sorry, that's up to you.

Spell Check
Microsoft Word has it, and lots of writers use that software, but the spell check function often won't catch the right use of words such as "their" or "they're" or "there." Still, it's a place to start and it's not a bad idea to run your chapters through spell check. One thing that infuriates some editors: Putting two spaces after a sentence. One space is plenty. Don't worry about it as you write, but do a search and replace for that during the editing stage.

NOTE:
Here's another tip: If you're reading for pleasure and you come across a word you don't know, stop and look it up. Put it in your words and phrases notebook. You'll learn something, and who knows when it might come in handy down the literary road. Also, keep a thesaurus nearby, use the one that comes with Microsoft Word, or find a better one online.

Out of Town Words

"If you open a book and find that the writer is trying to impress you with his knowledge of long, unusual words or by his use of foreign phrases, close the book quickly with no sense of loss or of deficiency or of having missed anything; for the author has not learned how to write and perhaps never will, and there is no need for you to offer yourself as a sounding board for his incompetence."
— **Burton Rascoe**, *literary critic and newspaperman*

We recommend keeping esoteric words to a minimum, unless you're trying to impress the hell out of your reader with your knowledge of the language.

Same goes for foreign words, ne c'est pas? Some readers will know what that French phrase means, is it not so? But others may not, and what we're trying to do here is to avoid stopping the reader cold while he or she ponders the meaning of a word or phrase, or worse yet, actually stops reading to go look it up. It's OK for you to do that as you read, but don't put the brakes on the average reader of your novel.

After you've written two or three readable novels, you may want to up your game, but not yet.

Dictation

"What really knocks me out is a book that, when you're all done reading it, you wish the author that wrote it was a terrific friend of yours and you could call him up on the phone whenever you felt like it. That doesn't happen much, though."
— **J.D. Salinger**

A lot of mediocre books these days, particularly mysteries and romance novels, seem to have been dictated, then run through an editing program or two, then self-published electronically. The result is that there is a lot of trash writing out there. Some people have even specialized in this, cranking out dozens if not hundreds of pretty crappy books.

Dictation can probably be made to work, with practice, if you're exceptionally good, and if you can be a crackerjack editor when it comes to your own prose. Almost everyone thinks faster than they can write, and dictating lets you erupt with words.

There are quite a few dictation applications available out there, and they can ease things a lot, once they "learn" your voice. These programs use speech recognition technology to convert spoken words to text. They're not only convenient but also speed up the rate at which text is entered. Depending on your writing style, that could be either good or bad. Dragon products are at the top of the market, but again, just do an online search for "dictation software."

Technology can be helpful, but it won't write your novel for you, and you probably wouldn't want to read it if it did. There really are no great shortcuts. You just have to sit down and do the work.

NOTE:
 However you write—computer, longhand, dictation, typewriter—read it aloud back to yourself. You'll find where the cadence is off, where you need a comma to allow a breathing space, where something just sounds awkward. If you're self-conscious about that, find a place where you can't be overheard. But try it.

Style

"If it sounds like writing, I rewrite it. Or, if proper usage gets in the way, it may have to go. I can't allow what we learned in English composition to disrupt the sound and rhythm of the narrative."
— **Elmore Leonard**

Ah yes, subjects, verbs, objects, adverbs, adjectives. They all work together to create style. At first, you may not have a style of your own. But as you write more, one will probably develop. Casual, fun-seeking? Serious, melancholy? Terse, but straight-forward?

As you read (and you should read constantly) make mental notes of the various styles. Robert Parker's style is so vastly different from Elmore Leonard's style that you might think they came from two different planets.

Think of a writer you like. Then try to write a paragraph describing their style. Just thinking about style helps you to develop your own. But don't copy someone else, or you run the risk of it sounding like parody.

Try to develop a basic, conversational style. Everyone is different, with different life experiences, so put yours to work. But write the way people around you talk. Different characters can talk differently. And unless you're as good as Mark Twain, stay away from dialect. It'll get you in trouble.

Titles

"When you boil it down, a title is a business decision."
— **Bethany Atazadeh**

Yep, you're going to need one. But don't worry too much about it in the early stages. Paul McCartney's hit song, "Yesterday" was titled "Scrambled Eggs" in the first draft, but it got better. Chances are your title will come to you as you write, so don't sweat it too much.

But it would be nice eventually to come up with something memorable that relates to the overall theme of your book.

GoodReads dot com users voted Philip K. Dick's "Do Androids Dream of Electric Sheep" as one of the best titles of all time. The movie "Blade Runner" was based on that short story.

You can think of a title as a window into the soul of your book, working in concert with the cover drawing or photograph. Your aim is to intrigue the reader, get him or her to open the book, read the blurb or click on the image. It is, in effect, advertising.

"Titles are important; I have them before I have books that belong to them."
— **John Irving**

The Writing Community

"...writers' peer groups ... They're a wonderful invention. They put the writer into a community of people all working at the same art, the kind of group musicians and painters and dancers have always had."
— **Ursula K. Le Guin**

Writers groups come and go. Their value is debatable. But if you want to join an online community of writers, check out NaNoWriMo. It's free to join and who knows, they just might help you find inspiration.

NaNoWriMo says it "believes in the transformational power of creativity. We provide the structure, community, and encouragement to help people find their voices, achieve creative goals, and build new worlds—on and off the page."

Of course, there are other online groups. Facebook has a bunch of them, including one that has more than 130,000 members.

Then there is Scribophile and CritiqueCircle. And lots of others. A few minutes spent doing online searches may be helpful.

You could also join a local writers group— most cities have one or more. Again, just do a search online. But be cautious. Over the years, we've found local groups to be somewhat encouraging, but also less helpful than you might imagine— populated by lots of wannabe writers who are more socializers than serious authors. Your mileage may vary, as they say.

But ask yourself if your time might be better spent actually writing.

List your characters

"I want, even for the worst of the characters, grace under pressure, some slinking nobility."
—***Cormac McCarthy***

Even before you start outlining, you might want to consider a list of characters. This allows you to write a brief description of everyone in your novel, from the hero on down to the bad guys and right on through to the ancillary folks. Keep it separate from the outline, so you can easily add descriptions of each person as additional ideas occur to you.

The character list will allow you to go back and make sure that you have cohesion throughout the text, assuring that you don't describe someone as a blonde in one chapter and then call her a brunette five chapters later. That may sound silly, but it's easy to get lost in 100,000-plus or more words in your manuscript— especially since you won't ever be able to see it all on one page or one screen.

Creating a list like this allows you some time to think about your characters.

In addition to a physical description and relationship to the other characters, you can also provide each character with some motivation. The last thing you want your reader to do is come to a screeching halt, wondering why would this person do that?

Flow is always important. Think of your book as a river. Don't put up unnecessary dams.

The Heart of the Matter

"The hard part about writing a novel is finishing it."
— *Ernest Hemingway*

The Form of an Outline

Many of us were taught back in grade school or junior high how to construct a classic outline, using Roman numerals, Arabic numerals and upper case and lower case letters.

Something like this, just as an example:

VII
(Chapter Seven)

A. Here's what this chapter is all about
1
Setting the scene — locale.
a
Maybe something you don't want to forget.
b. A memory of how the tree tops stuck out of the fog, like multiple smoke funnels on an old-fashioned cruise ship.
2
Description of the good guys and the bad guys.
a. Some dialogue. So-and-so says "xxx."
B.
Introduction to the action. Something happens. Maybe just a few words to describe it: The action was like a meth-fueled, late-night liquor store hold-up.

That form of outline is all well and good, and if you only want to rough out your story, it might suffice. You will have to keep the bulk of what you want to do in your head, however. There probably are some Pantsers who use brief little outlines like that, and more power to them if it works. Some folks even use storyboards, tacked to a wall, so they can look up at their outline as they write.

We don't know whether he's a Pantser, but we were intrigued by the outlines that Cormac McCarthy put in front of every chapter of his novel "Blood Meridian."

For example, this from Chapter 9: "An ambuscade – The dead Apache – Hollow ground – A gypsum lake – Trebillones – Snow-blind horses – The Delawares return – A probate – The ghost coach – The copper mines – Squatters – A snakebit horse – The judge on geological evidence –The dead boy – On parallax and false guidance in things past – The ciboleros"

Trebillones are dust spouts. Ciboleros are Mexican buffalo hunters of the 1850s. That book is no beach read, and people either love it or hate it, but it does have some marvelous sentences in it, like this one: "The mountains in their blue islands stood footless in the void like floating temples."

If you're not a Pantser and you want to write a novel with some heft to it, with some ideas worth considering, with some intriguing characters in an interesting locale doing scary or heroic things, you're going to have to put some meat on the bones of your outline. Feel free to write complete sentences in your outline. You may be able to copy whole sentences later on. Outlining in more depth means that portions of your outline can be incorporated right into the manuscript.

And if you do that, you may almost find yourself "writing by the numbers."

NOTE:
Nowadays most people write on computers, so it's easy to cut and paste. So, simply copy the outline for each chapter to the beginning of each chapter. That way, if you get a little lost in the writing, you can just scroll up a little and refresh yourself on how you originally envisioned that chapter. No need to jump back and forth between screens., or scroll back 100 pages.

Epigraph

"I had to lay one brick on another, set millions of words to paper before writing one real, authentic word dragged up from my own guts."
— **Henry Miller**

An epigraph is a quote or maybe a saying or short proverb at the beginning of a novel. They are sometimes used at the beginning of each chapter. That's nice, but it adds some extra work to find the perfect little relevant quote.

If you were writing a book that included a shipwreck, for example, you might use as an epigraph a modified quote from Shakespeare:

"Full fathom five thy father lies ...
... Those are pearls that were his eyes..."
— **Shakespeare**, *The Tempest*

Or, for a novel that features a ghost, or a reference to ghosts:

"The muddy rumors
Of your burial move me
To half-believe ... your reappearance"
— **Sylvia Plath**

An epigraph is not always the best place to start, but rather is something to consider when your novel is complete and you have a feel for what you have written.

Prologue

"Nothing any good isn't hard."
— F. Scott Fitzgerald

Many, many novels have no epigraph, but they may well start with a prologue. It's not a requirement, and you can simply just start with Chapter One if you like. Lots of books do.

A prologue is the beginning of a story that establishes some context and gives background details and/or some back-story that ties into the main plot. It can also be used to set a scene or a locale, paint a picture of a character or two and pique the reader's interest.

It's an opportunity for the writer to give the reader a heads-up, to say, hey, this is another in a series about Amos Ace, Private Eye, who operates out of Whatever City, USA and lives in a McMansion with his aging mother and has a semi-serious problem with depression.

That can work well for the second or umpteenth novel in a series featuring the same main character or characters. But if it's your first attempt, or if it features new characters, it's not really necessary.

The first sentence – or sentences

"We write to taste life twice, in the moment and in retrospect."
— *Anais Nin*

Critical or not, we can debate the point endlessly. But it seems clear that an appealing opening sentence or two or three in the prologue or in Chapter 1 is helpful to draw in the reader by setting the scene or introducing an action or character that makes one want to keep going.

Consider this, from "The Prince of Tides" by **Pat Conroy**:

"My wound is geography. It is also my anchorage, my port of call."

We soon learn that the geography is that of the South Carolina Low Country, where the narrator grew up. It is beautifully described and in many ways, throughout the book, it is one of the principal characters, if only in a metaphorical sense.

And, for one of the all-time best opening sentences in a book, check out **Hunter S. Thompson's** "Fear and Loathing in Las Vegas" in which he writes:

"We were somewhere around Barstow on the edge of the desert when the drugs began to take hold. I remember saying something like `I feel a bit lightheaded; maybe you should drive ...' And suddenly there was a terrible roar all around us and the sky was full of what looked like huge bats, all swooping and screeching and diving around the car, which was going about a hundred miles an hour with the top down to Las Vegas."

Geeze, how can you not keep reading?

Still, while it is important, don't get stuck on writing that perfect first sentence—it may come later, much later, during the editing phase. Just start writing. You don't want to freeze on that first sentence.

White Space / Line Space

"...instead of telling us a thing was 'terrible,' describe it so that we'll be terrified. Don't say it was 'delightful,' make us say 'delightful' when we've read the description."
— **C.S. Lewis**

One trick that some writers use to provide separation of disparate sections inside the same chapter is simply to insert a line or two of white space. In other words, you don't need to start a new chapter every time the scene changes. This works best if the various sections are somewhat related, especially if they are occurring at more or less the same time or involve some of the main characters, even if not the protagonist.

Chapter Titles or Numbers

Hey, it's completely up to you.

Starting your outline

"When writing a novel, that's pretty much entirely what life turns into: 'House burned down. Car stolen. Cat exploded. Did 1500 easy words, so all in all it was a pretty good day."
— Neil Gaiman

OK, this is really simple, so just do it. Open a new file on your computer or just use a long legal pad.

Remember, what follows is the form, or skeleton, of your novel. It's up to you to make it readable, to make someone want to read it, to keep their interest going.

The truth is, you need to be creative, both with your plots and characters and with your choice of words for action and description. Sorry, but that's just the way it is. You need to do the heavy lifting. And, if you're writing on a computer, don't forget to back up your work. Frequently. And do it in the cloud, or off-site in case the house burns down.

So let's get down to it. You can use what follows as a template if you like. Modify it to best suit your needs. Simplify it. Expand it or contract it. But do start working on your novel with some sort of outline.

Prologue

"The most powerful words in English are 'Tell me a story...'"
— ***Pat Conroy***

Just as an example, we're going to outline a mystery novel that we recently read and liked very much, both for the writing and its organization. It was a complicated read, but we never got lost.

We'll start by discussing a prologue. Remember, you can do a prologue if you want, but it's not necessary.

A prologue (or Chapter 1) should introduce one or more of the characters—people who will show up later in the text. It doesn't always have to introduce the main character— it could introduce some ancillary characters, or some of the bad guys, or it can even be an action, or something that introduces a character and features some action. Clearly, it should be interesting. You want the reader to keep turning those pages.

Your prologue (or first Chapter 1) can be anywhere from one to a half-dozen or more pages, but try to end it in such a way that the reader wants to keep going. In fact, that's a good way to end any chapter.

One book we recently edited had a short prologue that helped the reader to reference some of the things that happened in a previous novel involving the same characters.

Chapter 1 then featured the main character at a stake-out, and ended with a gargantuan explosion. We got to know a little about the main character and were intrigued by the blast, which took out a radio preacher and a drag queen. Cameras, drones, freezing cold, all were part of the scene.

But that's not the only way to start a book. The sci fi writer **William Gibson** will often write three or four different chapters, none of which seem related at the beginning of the book, but which coalesce as you keep reading. It's a great technique, but again, we don't recommend it for beginners.

Chapter 1

"... write what it is you think your story is about. You discover new characters, add little thumbnail sketches of them; you make notes about the feeling you want to get here and there. You create the whole book out of bulleted phrases and sentences, paragraphs and maybe even flowcharts. Finally the day will arrive when you come to the end of the outline."
—*Walter Mosley*

Or just start with Chapter 1. Prologue or no, you should introduce the main character, or some other characters. Give the characters a little back-story, but not too much—there will be plenty of time for more description later. Don't worry too much about a physical description of the main character, especially if it's a first-person novel. A little description may help, but you don't need to list every scar or mole.

However, learning to describe secondary characters in two or three sentences is a talent that will stand you in good stead as you go along. Think of it as writing word portraits.

You should establish the time period, if you can do it easily. If it's current day, just assume it, if not, sneak it in someplace unobtrusively. Same with the weather. We've all experienced weather, so it immediately gives the reader something to relate to. And yeah, you can end a sentence with a preposition. Don't let anybody tell you differently.

OK, the outline for Chapter 1 (and all the other chapters) should include all of what you want it to do, and some of what you want the characters to say.

Do it in the classic outline form if you like:

Chapter I

1. Ask yourself, what do I want to accomplish here. Set the scene.
A. Introduce the main character.
a. Describe the main character a bit.
B. Describe the locale. Don't set your book in San Diego if you've never been there.
C. Introduce a secondary character, describe him or her, including faults.
a. Maybe a quote here.
D. Maybe describe how the faults relate to the main character.
E. Introduce the bad guys and describe them a little.
a. Bad guy No. 1
b. Bad guy No. 2
F. Have the bad guys do something bad.
G. End with some sort of surprise action or a teaser, something to make the reader want to keep going. That's not a requirement, and don't struggle with it if it doesn't come naturally in the narrative, but it's helpful.

You can expand under each of the letters above, putting flesh on the bones, adding some dialogue, some description, etc—but try to keep in mind how this opening is going to relate to the rest of your book. Feel free to copy this format.

You don't have to start at the beginning, but it's never a bad place to start.

For example, the mystery novel we are referencing here skipped a prologue, but started in Chapter 1 by introducing the main character (male), in a beautifully described Florida locale, and included some of the main character's flaws (alcoholism.) It also introduced a character who becomes a friend of the main character, who also has flaws— a gambling problem. The secondary character ends up getting killed in a shootout at a robbery engineered by some loan sharks to whom he owes money. All this in about 15 pages that include a description of where these events took place, when, what the weather was, some background on the main protagonist, a little about his friend, and brief descriptions of the loan shark and his enforcers.

It's a perfect setup for a novel about the hunt for the killers, but wait, you have to move forward 20 years— to the present day—to see how it all comes out. That's a neat little twist.

Chapter 2

"What happens next is the thing that keeps people reading, and the more important the next [thing is], then the more important the work is."
— **John D. MacDonald**, *author of the Travis McGee series*

Same book. We want to get back to the main character and flesh out the protagonist a bit. We add a little description— not so much physical description, more like telling the reader who the person is, their background, what influences have shaped them.

Keep in mind that anywhere in your outline, you are free to write in snatches of dialog, descriptions of locale or characters, and what the weather was.

Introduce some secondary characters. Maybe the protagonist's friends, or boss, or underlings or siblings. Describe them. Have them do something, like offering advice to the main character, or interacting some other way, maybe threatening him or her.

And make something else happen to keep the plot moving. Maybe another murder. Maybe something or somebody does something related to the action in the prologue or in Chapter 1. Maybe it's something entirely new.

Outline it all. All the new characters, how they relate to each other, how they move the story along, or how they meander down into entertaining dead ends.

Use line breaks (a line of white space) if it feels right.

You can structure your outline any way you want, from rigid format to loosey-goosey, complete with narrative and quotes, or not. Feel free to pick an outline style that works for you. But remember, you always want to be able to come back to the outline for guidance on the direction that your story is heading. It's easy to get sidetracked while in the writing "zone."

Here, in a simplified fashion, is how our mystery story was organized over about 20 pages in Chapter 2:

1. A section that moves the reader gracefully from the events in Chapter 1 into the present day. Explains how the murder in Chapter 1 was never solved. Basically three long paragraphs. No dialogue.

2. A section that further describes the protagonist (a male cop, we'll call him Hero) and introduces another character (female) who is the Daughter of the Murder Victim in Chapter 1. This character is introduced in a casino setting. This woman may be laundering recently stolen money from a bank heist. This character turns out to be pivotal later. We'll call her Pivotal Daughter.

3. A section that introduces a good-guy character (the Sheriff, who is a woman), and takes the Hero and the Sheriff to the scene of the apparent suicide of a teen-age girl. We'll call her Suicide Girl. Great description of the Sheriff. Description of the locale. Description of the body and the surrounding area. Some dialogue between Hero and the Sheriff. They interview some witnesses. Interview Father of Suicide Girl. Obtain Suicide Girl's diary. More dialogue.

4. A section about Pivotal Daughter, in which our Hero and the Sheriff have some dialogue. The reader learns how Pivotal Daughter relates to the happenings in Chapter 1.

5. A section describing how the Hero goes home, describes his house, wife, neighbors, where he lives, etc. Dialogue with Hero and his wife. Some shared affection, but no sex. Speculation about the suicide. A brief primer on suicide, how it's done, how men and women tend to do it differently.

NOTE:
As you write, don't be afraid to make observations about things that are relevant to the story — maybe the traffic, how storms are created, your hero's martial arts training. Just make them somewhat

relevant to the narrative. For this kind of book, there's no need to go off on a political rant or an essay about saving the environment. Mention it if you like, but keep in mind that your reader wants to be entertained, not lectured to. (See, you can indeed end a sentence with a preposition. And the Earth is still turning.)

6. Dialogue with the Coroner. Word portrait of the Coroner, who is an asshole. Description of the suicide, cause of death, etc. Some friction between Hero and the Coroner.
7. A call from the crime lab.
8. Introduction of a new character, FBI Agent. Description of agent, who mentions a possible crime involving Pivotal Daughter.
9. Exploration of Suicide Girl's diary. Description of diary. Very feminine. Introduction of new, but unnamed character, Son of Prominent Citizen.

NOTE:
Each new character is described in word portraits as they are introduced in the narrative. Some are more flattering than others. Also, this chapter is almost all first person. But the next one won't be, it will alternate between first and third person, as described earlier.

And, keep in mind that this is a somewhat bare-bones outline. Your creativity and writing talent come into play as you flesh out the characters, describe the action and drive the plot forward. Feel free to plug bits of description and dialogue into the outline. Every time you do that, it will make the actual writing of that section faster and easier.

Chapter 3

"In my opinion, one of the biggest secrets of suspense is setting up questions that the readers must have answered."
—**James Patterson**

1. Hero visits the apartment of Pivotal Daughter from Chapter 2. Description of apartment complex. Dialogue with her. We meet some of her friends. Word portraits of the friends. Guy who looks like a jockey. Guy who looks like a boxer. Guy who says he is an actor. Woman who says she's an aspiring country singer. All are secondary characters. Lots of dialogue.

2. Hero returns to office. Begins to work on another unsolved case, a hit and run. Accident or homicide? At this point, no apparent relationship to Suicide Girl. But there will be, later in the book. Description of the hit-and-run victim, where his body was found, how long ago, etc. Hero talks to Coroner about the case. Discrepancies in the autopsy. Coroner gets huffy. Dialogue. More conversation with FBI Agent. More description of agent. More dialogue.

Chapter 4

"Lots of people can write a good first page but to sustain it, that's my litmus test. If I flip to the middle of the book and there's a piece of dialogue that's just outstanding, or a description, then I'll flip back to the first page and start it."
—**Carl Hiaasen**

1. Hero goes home. A reading of Suicide Girl's diary. Portions of diary quoted verbatim. Conversation with Hero's wife. Bit of an argument.

2. Hero wakes up at 2 a.m. Hero thinks it's not a suicide.

3. Next day, Hero visits home of Prominent Citizen. Why? Suicide Girl had worked for Prominent Citizen. Description of home, description of locale, explanation of Prominent Citizen's odd name, details about the man's family background. Prominent Citizen has an ownership interest in a casino. Casino? Yes, it's a hint. More conversation. They discuss the suicide. Some harsh words are exchanged.

4. Long section. Introduction of a completely new character, the Best Friend of our Hero. This is a third-person section. Lots of description of this character's background, work history, motivations. This section segues seamlessly into a first-person conversation with our Hero. Yes, the casino comes up again. Big time. The Pivotal Female is involved in some grifter action at the casino.

Chapter 5

"You can get help from teachers, but you are going to have to learn a lot by yourself, sitting alone in a room."
—**Dr. Seuss**

1. Opens with a section in which Hero thinks abut drinking (he has a drinking problem still) and the use of drugs, moves into a third-person description of the Prominent Citizen's Son and how Son, a college kid, gets into a fight with some low-level drug dealers at a fast-food restaurant. One of the drug dealers becomes a central character (we'll call him Drug Dealer), as does the Son of the Prominent Citizen and the son's college student friend, who is the Son of a Mob Boss. Detailed description of the confrontation. The Drug Dealer gets pistol-whipped by the Son of a Mob Boss —the Mob Boss who figured in Chapter 1. Gunplay is threatened. Dialogue between the characters as tempers flare. There is violence. This scene pits black youths against the white college kids.

2. Next section is first person. Hero is dispatched to the scene of the confrontation, which is still going on. A crowd has gathered. There is an expository section on the nature of violence in society. Our hero warns Prominent Citizen's Son. Son of the Mob Boss is arrested for assault on Drug Dealer.

3. Another first person section that begins by discussing Hero's drinking problem and how it has affected him over the years. Hero meets the Mob Boss and his Hired Muscle at a restaurant. Dialogue. Mob Boss complains about the arrest of his son and how the Drug Dealer threatened his son with a gun. Hired Muscle has nasty words with Hero.

4. Hero returns to office, runs Mob Boss's name through national crime records, as well as name of Hired Muscle. Gets a hit on Hired Muscle. Finds a psychological profile of Hired Muscle, done while he was in prison. Section segues into a long-ish exposition of the locale where Hero lives and its history of crime. Pins the Mob Boss to financial interests in casinos and brothels.

Chapter 6

"Writing is not necessarily something to be ashamed of, but do it in private and wash your hands afterwards."
—**Robert A. Heinlein**

By now you should be getting the general idea.

1. More on FBI Agent introduced earlier. Description. Dialogue with Hero. Turns out FBI Agent is working on a case involving Mob Boss.

2. A new section that elaborates on the unsolved hit-and-run that may or may not be a homicide. It will turn out to be related to the main plot as we go along.

3. Hero interviews Drug Dealer. Expository section on how the dope trade works at the lower levels. Hero warns Drug Dealer not to take revenge on Son of the Mob Boss. Lots of dialogue.

4. A dream sequence. Involves the casino and some of the characters we've been introduced to. Turns out Suicide Girl was wearing a T-shirt with the casino logo.

5. Hero visits home of Prominent Citizen again, but father isn't there. His son is. Lots of dialogue. Does Son of Prominent Citizen know the suicide? Hmmm, yes.

6. Hero goes fishing with his wife and Best Friend. Turns out Best Friend has a date later with Pivotal Daughter. Lots of dialogue.

Chapter 7

"I was convinced that the only thing I wanted to do ever — was write novels."
—*J. K. Rowling*

1. Drug Dealer who was beaten up earlier files charges against the Son of the Mob Boss. Dialogue with hero.

2. Son of Mob Boss arrested. Roughed up by arresting officers, because he's a real snot.

3. Hero focuses on other cases.

4. Hero visits home of Drug Dealer. Dialogue. Warns Drug Dealer that Mob Boss will retaliate.

5. Drug Dealer gives hero a tip on the hit-and-run mentioned earlier.

6. Hero visits auto repair shop in response to tip. Learns who brought in a car damaged in the accident – surprise, it was the Prominent Citizen.

7. Prominent Citizen visits Hero at home. They have angry words. Turns out Suicide Girl had been dating Son of the Prominent Citizen, who says his son's life was threatened by Drug Dealer, following that fight at the restaurant.

Chapter 8

"I wanted to see my name on the cover of a book. If your name is in the Library of Congress, you're immortal."
—**Tom Clancy**

1. More details on the hit-and-run victim. Dialogue with crime lab guy. Maybe the hit-and-run was not the cause of death. Evidence points to Prominent Citizen.

2. Hero meets with District Attorney, who tells Hero to back off investigating Prominent Citizen.

3. Prominent Citizen is arrested in connection with hit-and-run. His Son is also dragged out of class in handcuffs, but not arrested. Hero takes Son to a remote spot and "encourages" him to implicate his father in the hit-and-run. The possibility is raised that the hit-and-run was done by the Prominent Citizen's wife.

4. Hero meets up with Best Friend. Dialogue. Best Friend defends dating Pivotal Daughter.

There are 19 more chapters, leading up to the last chapter. Many, many beach-read mystery novels, or adventure novels, or romance novels, or fantasy novels convey to the reader a steady upwelling of plot, leading to the last chapter, or penultimate chapter, where the action comes to an exciting conclusion, sometimes including violence, in which all is revealed and resolved.

Chapter 27

"Writing is the product of a deeply disturbed psyche, and is by no means therapeutic."
—**Edna O'Brien**

By now you've got the basic idea of a very simple outline. You really don't need all those letters and Roman numerals, but it wouldn't hurt if you wanted to try it that way. We prefer the straightforward approach, No. 1 through No. xxx.

This is the last chapter, the one with the most action, the one with the resolution of all, or almost all of the various plot points.
It goes like this:

1. Hero arms himself with guns, including a sawed-off shotgun.
2. Hero tells wife he has to go out to save Best Friend, because he thinks friend is in danger. Wife begs him not to go. He goes anyway, of course.
3. Hero drives out to meet Father of Suicide Girl. Dialogue. The Father admits to some crimes. But Hero knows he's basically a good guy. Lots of gray areas here. Father now believes Son of Prominent Citizen drove his daughter to kill herself.
4. They drive together down to an old hunting cabin in the woods.
5. Hero tells the Father to wait in car and approaches cabin.
6. Hero finds Best Friend's car burned out, with an unrecognizable body inside. Description of body. Much angst. Is it Best Friend? We don't know. Hero thinks it is.
7. Hero sneaks up to the cabin. Description of his progress through the woods.
8. Hero enters back door of cabin, shotgun in hand.
9. Hero finds Pivotal Daughter (Daughter of the Murder Victim in the first chapter) hogtied on the floor. Best Friend is gagged and tied to a chair. He has been tortured. Turns out Pivotal Daughter had been running an elaborate ruse to get the FBI to bring down the Mob Boss. (That had been explained earlier)
10. Mob Boss's hit man (Hired Muscle) is there, with a gun. Hero shoots him immediately in the throat. Description of blood spatter on

the wallpaper. Best friend can't talk, but nods in the direction of a door to a bedroom.

11. Mob Boss comes out shooting. Hero is wounded but fires second barrel of shotgun. Catches Mob Boss in the gut. Best Friend mumbles something unintelligible through the gag and keeps nodding at the bedroom. But clearly Hero thinks he's nailed all the bad guys.

12. Hero reaches in pocket for cell phone to call for help before untying Best Friend.

13. Wife of Prominent Citizen appears in bedroom doorway with small pistol. Hero realizes no more shells in the shotgun. Dialogue between the two. She tells him she is the brains behind everything. She admits to being the driver in the hit-and-run killing. Says it was simply an accident, but it had to be covered up. More dialogue, aimed at wrapping up loose ends of the mystery.

14. She raises gun and points it at Hero's face. There's a gunshot from behind Hero, catching the Wife in the face. Shot was fired by Father of Girl Who Killed Herself, who was told to wait in the car, but didn't.

15. Hero calls the cops and the FBI.

Epilogue

"There is no real ending. It's just the place where you stop the story."
— Frank Herbert

1. Best Friend explains what happened from his point of view. He was locked in trunk of car. Found a flare pistol, the kind boaters carry. Got out of trunk, shot one of the bad guys. Car caught fire and blew up. Bad guy burned to death, but Best Friend was caught by Mob Boss and Hired Muscle.
2. Father of Girl who Killed Herself pleads guilty to the earlier murder of Son of Prominent Citizen, as he came to blame him for his daughter's suicide. He's portrayed as a good guy, but he goes to prison for life.
3. Son of Mob Boss skates.
4. Hints of really bad weather coming. A little hint about the next book in the series?
5. Some expository prose on the nature of life, the nature of evil and the nature of randomness. The end.

OK, get writing

"The worst enemy to creativity is self-doubt."
— **Sylvia Plath**

So, there's an example of how to outline your novel. You can fill it with your material and use it as a guide for your book. When you get stuck, or confused, or uncertain— and you probably will— you'll have something concrete you can consult to get you back on the right track.

So, like they say at Nike, just do it!

"A writer who waits for ideal conditions under which to work will die without putting a word on paper."
— **EB White**

Don't feel like it?

Do it anyway.

Do something.

One sentence.

There, didn't that feel good?

Keep Going

"Ultimately you write alone. And ultimately you and you alone can judge your work. The judgment that a work is complete — this is what I meant to do, and I stand by it — can come only from the writer, and it can be made rightly only by a writer who's learned to read her own work. Group criticism is great training for self-criticism. But until quite recently no writer had that training, and yet they learned what they needed. They learned it by doing it."
— **Ursula K. Le Guin**

Turn your phone off. Minimize interruptions. As the famous sports writer Red Smith allegedly once said (it's been paraphrased a zillion times and the attribution is iffy):
"Writing is easy. You just sit there and sweat blood."

Caution: We're writing here, not editing. Feel free to look back over your work a bit, but don't get bogged down in details. It's OK if you misspell "accommodate." That will get fixed in the editing and proofing stages.

And don't get distracted while writing your book.

In the words of **Henry Miller**:
"Work on one thing at a time until finished."

First Draft Done?

"... plumb the comedy, honor the pain, shape the story as honestly and beautifully as you can."
— **Cynthia D'Aprix Sweeney**, *author of "The Nest"*

Whew! There you did it. Congrats!

Now what?

You may not want to hear this, but ... your work is just beginning.

Read that one more time: Your work is just beginning.

Time to move into the editing phase.

What's That Mean?

"...you should say what you mean," the March Hare went on.
"I do," Alice hastily replied. "At least— at least I mean what I say— that's the same thing, you know."
"Not the same thing a bit!" said the Mad Hatter. "You might just as well say that 'I see what I eat' is the same thing as 'I eat what I see!'"
—**Lewis Carroll**, *Alice's Adventures in Wonderland*

So, now you have a first draft. It's always a good idea to have two or three other people read your manuscript, not so much to edit it but more to give you some advice on where things can be improved, where sections are too wordy, or places where everything came to a full stop. That last is what you really want to avoid, especially in what folks call a "popular novel."

Tell your readers not to spare the criticism and to be honest. Did you like it? Was it boring? Exciting? Too complex? Too simple? Unrealistic? Derivative? How about the ending? Did you like or hate the characters? What did you think about the style?

You don't have to take their advice. Remember, everybody has an opinion. What you're looking for is a new way of seeing your own work by putting yourself in the reader's brain.

The Editing Process
or Sweetheart, Get Me Rewrite

"If a sentence, no matter how excellent, does not illuminate your subject in some new and useful way, scratch it out."
—**Kurt Vonnegut**

Unless you're an incredibly talented Pantser, a lot of your writing work will be done in the editing phase.

"When you write a book, you spend day after day scanning and identifying the trees. When you're done, you have to step back and look at the forest."
— **Stephen King**

And you should seriously edit your own work. And then edit it again. Just running your manuscript through spell check is not nearly enough. But it will catch a few mistakes and is useful for eliminating double spaces between words and sentences. Like we said, that's one of those little things that drive editors crazy.

"More often than not if I've done nine pages I may be able to save two and a half or three," poet and writer **Maya Angelou** once told the Paris Review. *"That's the cruelest time you know."*

It is easy to fall in love with a nice sentence you've written that doesn't contribute to moving the story along. Dump it.

Here's an example of what an editor can do to save you from yourself:

Someone wrote "She lifted her coffee from the cup holder and took a couple of strong sips."

The editor suggested: "She sipped her coffee." At times you may find yourself padding your manuscript with extra words just to make it longer. Don't do that.

On editing and rewriting your own work, the late **Toni Morrison** has been quoted as saying:
"It's not that you're changing it: you're doing it better, hitting a higher note or a deeper tone or a different color. The revision for me is the exciting part; it's the part that I can't wait for—getting the whole damn thing done so that I can do the real work, which is making it better and better and better."

And then, after you've been over it all a few times, find an editor, tell them what you want and pay what they ask. It takes a lot of years and experience to become a good editor, and if you are lucky enough to find one that you can afford, go for it. Sure, a friend can read over what you have written, and maybe even offer some good advice. But a talented, experienced editor can explain the why behind recommended changes. He or she can even make you see things in a new light, influencing you to write better in the future.

Whether you're writing novels, nonfiction, short stories or articles for a newspaper or magazine, you need someone who can help. It's not a cliché that everyone needs an editor.

An editor can do everything from the basics of correcting spelling and grammar to rewriting entire manuscripts.

A good editor will give you a fresh perspective on your work, gently point out where things could be improved and encourage you to keep getting better and better.

An excellent editor can do all that and more.

As **Mark Twain** once said, *"the difference between the almost right word and the right word is ... the difference between the lightning bug and the lightning."*

There are three types of editing:

There's the quick look-over, in essence a proof-reading, looking for typographical errors and those silly instances when you may have written "their" when you meant "they're." Yeah, English is tough that way. Many spell-check programs are going to look at that and say, "hey, looks good to me," and unless someone catches it, it will make you look as if English is not your strong point.

Then there's a good copy editing, which does everything in the look-over and more, such as pointing out a lack of first references, inconsistencies of character in word and deed, logical impossibilities, subject-verb agreement— the basics of a decent editing job.

And finally there's a thorough editing, which does all of the above AND provides the author with well thought out suggestions for improving the story, maybe by adding or deleting whole sections, suggesting alternative words, asking questions, making sure there's nothing in the manuscript that stops the reader cold. This kind of editor works directly with the writer, preferably face-to-face, so that suggested changes can be discussed in detail. The writer, of course, has final say, but a really top-notch editor is, in essence, a partner.

Marketing Your Book

"A written book-marketing and promotion plan will give you a blueprint for promoting your book and keep you focused on what's important."
— **Dana Lynn Smith**

Here's the good news: Genre fiction generally sells better than literary or mainstream fiction, because it has a readership that has more or less pre-selected itself. That's why books in stores are sold in various sections, from romance to mystery to sci fi. After all, you probably know what you like.

Entire books have been written on the subject of marketing books, and you probably should read a few of them. Amazon has a bunch of them. Just be sure to read the reviews before buying one. There are many options for writers today, from sending out query letters to established agents and book publishers to the various opportunities for self-publishing. Both Amazon and Smashwords immediately come to mind for the latter.

If you want to send out a query to a publisher or an agent, we recommend actually mailing a letter. Some folks get thousands of emails, and they are easily overlooked. An actual letter shows you put some effort into it.

Where to find an agent or publisher? Why, your trusty Internet search engine, of course. Just make sure you have your book finished. Otherwise, you're asking someone to bet on your dreams. Agents are good to have because they give you access to traditional publishers who don't accept unsolicited queries. On the other hand, it can be almost as hard to find the right agent as it is to find a traditional publisher. That's why self-published e-books are so popular.

Marketing your book— and turning a manuscript from a file on your computer into a real book, or an e-book, complete with cover, blurbs, dedication, etc— will take you some time, effort and probably some money.

We're not going to go into all that detail here (cleverly leaving room for us to write a follow-up to what you're reading), but we do have one piece of advice, and that is that people actually do judge a book by its cover. Therefore we strongly recommend that if you self-publish (nothing wrong with that, by the way) then be willing to pay for a really nice book cover by a good artist or graphics expert— a cover that will prompt a reader to pick up the book and browse a bit, or at the very least download the first 10 percent of an e-book.

Also, we recommend you pay someone to format your electronic book for you. Chances are you're a writer, not a tech wizard, and the different formats required by different web sites can be confusing. You're better off spending the time on an outline for your *next* book.

Do not — repeat NOT — fall into the trap of forking over large or even medium sums of money to people who claim they are able to turn your book into an overnight best-seller. These folks know how eager you are to get your book published, and they prey on your desires. They call it the vanity press for a reason.

And do NOT pay anyone for glowing reviews. That's cheating. Don't be a cheater. However, it's perfectly OK to send or give a copy of your book to a friend or an acquaintance and ask them for a review— an honest review.

You might also want to browse in a bookstore (there really are a few brick and mortar bookstores left) for books on marketing your manuscript.

Of course, you can also do a search online for literary agents and/or publishers that actually solicit manuscripts. But our advice is to run like hell if you come across anyone wanting to charge you money for looking at your book.

And be aware that if you decide to sell your book online, Amazon, Smashwords or whoever dot com will take a percentage of every sale ranging anywhere from 30 to 70 percent of the price.

There. You can't say you weren't warned.

And by the way, it's not a bad idea to copyright your work. Just go to copyright dot gov, the website set up by the Library of Congress. You'll find an online portal to register copyrights for photographs, sculptures and written works. Fill out the form, pay the fee and you are registered. At the time of this writing, the fee was only $65.

Other good books on writing

"If you are going to be a writer there is nothing I can say to stop you; if you're not going to be a writer nothing I can say will help you."
—**James Baldwin**

Miss Thistlebottom's Hobgoblins:
The Careful Writer's Guide to the Taboos, Bugbears, and Outmoded Rules of English Usage
By Theodore M. Bernstein

The Elements of Style
By William Strunk Jr. and E.B. White

The Associated Press Stylebook
Free on Amazon with a Kindle Unlimited membership
It's newspaper-y, but informative.

On Writing: A Memoir of the Craft
By Stephen King

Story Genius: How to Use Brain Science to Go Beyond Outlining and Write a Riveting Novel *(Before You Waste Three Years Writing 327 Pages That Go Nowhere)*
By Lisa Cron

Zen in the Art of Writing
By Ray Bradbury

The Magic of Fiction: Crafting Words into Story
By Beth Hill

Big Magic: Creative Living Beyond Fear
by Elizabeth Gilbert

Some good stuff here:
authorsguild.org

A few words on plagiarism

"Writing is a form of personal freedom. It frees us from the mass identity we see in the making all around us. In the end, writers will write not to be outlaw heroes of some underculture but mainly to save themselves, to survive as individuals."
—**Don Delillo**, *Harpers, April 1996*

Don't.

Just don't.

You'll get caught.

So don't.

Some thoughts about commas

"... I am a fan of the comma; it gives cadence to my writing. Those who disagree are in their usual hurried state ... not giving pause where a breath is due."
— **Nanette L. Avery**

We're not about teaching English usage here, but in our experience, a lot of beginning writers seem to have problems putting commas in the right places

The common comma can be a pesky little devil. Lowly and unimportant on the one hand, changing the meaning of a sentence or a phrase entirely on the other.

Generally speaking, it helps if you read your sentence aloud, or at least "aloud in your mind." You'll often see where a comma belongs, whether to give the reader a pause to breathe or to alter the meaning. Once you get it, the presence or absence of commas in the right places will become almost automatic.

Consider this short little sentence: "I'm trying Jack." One could read that to mean that someone is going to drink some Tennessee whiskey.

Or, "I'm trying, Jack." One can read that to mean someone is putting forth effort.

Makes a lot of difference. English, what a language, no?

Then there is the Oxford comma, generally defined as the final comma in a list of things. The jury is out on how necessary that comma is. A lot of folks leave it out. Either way, it matters little to us, so don't agonize over it. Chances are your editor will insert one when he or she decides a slight additional pause is necessary.

Sadly, there's also the comma splice. A comma splice is when two independent clauses are incorrectly joined by a comma to make one sentence. Don't do that. Make two sentences. At least for now. When you've earned your stripes as a writer and want to get fancy, you'll have more leeway to get creative and maybe break some rules. But not now.

Remember to hyphenate most compound adjectives. And as for semicolons, well, to hell with them. Use a dash. Or a period and start a new sentence.

Need a refresher on basic English? Try these books:

Perfect English Grammar: The Indispensable Guide to Excellent Writing and Speaking
By Grant Barrett

Actually, the Comma Goes Here: A Practical Guide to Punctuation
By Lucy Cripps

Is writing fiction worthwhile?

"Failures, repeated failures, are sign posts on the road to achievement. One fails forward toward success."
—C. S. Lewis

Half of full-time authors earn less than the federal poverty level of $12,488, according to a 2020 report from The Author's Guild. Literary authors are the hardest hit, experiencing a 46% drop in their book-related income in just five years.

The report cites the rise of Amazon's Kindle e-books, the decline of newspapers and the fact that more and more consumers are turning to their screens and to video.

The report goes on to say that 80 per cent of all authors earn less than what most people would consider a living wage. Authorhood is not a conventional, salary-paying career.

Still, it was the late author A.E. Hotchner who said:
"Of course we all have our limits, but how can you possibly find your boundaries unless you explore as far and as wide as you possibly can? I would rather fail in an attempt at something new and uncharted than safely succeed in a repeat of something I have (already) done."

So, don't give up.

"Write. There is no substitute ... But start small: write a good sentence, then a good paragraph, and don't be dreaming about writing the great American novel or what you'll wear at the awards ceremony because that's not what writing's about or how you get there from here. The road is made entirely out of words. Write a lot…it's effort and practice."
*—**Rebecca Solnit** on LitHub*

Maybe, or more likely probably, you'll need a source of support or an income stream of some sort as you go along. Few people, especially at first, have the luxury of doing nothing but working on a novel. But remember, if it's important enough to you, you can always set that alarm clock an hour early and get some prose down before you start your day.

Let's say it again.

Don't. Give. Up.

Remember:

"You fail only if you stop writing."
— **Ray Bradbury**

One More Thing

"Stay faithful to the stories in your head."
—**Paula Hawkins**

OK, this may or not be helpful, but here's another bare bones outline structure, condensed for you to use. Feel free to write it out and/or copy and paste.

Keep it simple. Set it up for each chapter if you like, with or without subheads. Feel free to use numbers instead of letters. Whatever. You don't need to overly complicate things.

Chapter 1
A. Ask yourself, what do I want to accomplish here. Set the overall scene.
B. Introduce the main character
C. Describe the locale. Don't set your book in San Diego if you've never been there.
D. Introduce a secondary character, describe him or her, including faults.
E. Describe how the faults relate to the main character.
F. Introduce the bad guys and describe them a little.
G. Have the bad guys do something bad.
Etc

Chapter 2
A. Overall, something happens.
B.
C.
Etc

Rinse and repeat for each chapter. Or use numbers rather than letters. And feel free to insert subheads. And description. Even dialogue.

"Not-writing is a good deal worse than writing."
— **Flannery O'Connor**, *The Habit of Being: Letters of Flannery O'Connor*

About the author

Beth Frances Cox worked as an editor at a half-dozen newspapers along the East Coast. One or two of them are still in business. She has edited everything from novels to technical manuals, as well as thousands of news articles about everything from riots to hurricanes. Always up for an adventure if it can be done sitting down, she is a sailor home from the sea and an occasional racecar driver.

Lastly

The author would like to extend special thanks to Cathy Diaz, Noreen Marcus and Ruth Thompson for their advice and encouragement.